Whore Secret

Hilarious Swear Word Coloring Book

For Fun & Stress Releasing

Charles C. Golden

Happy Coloring!

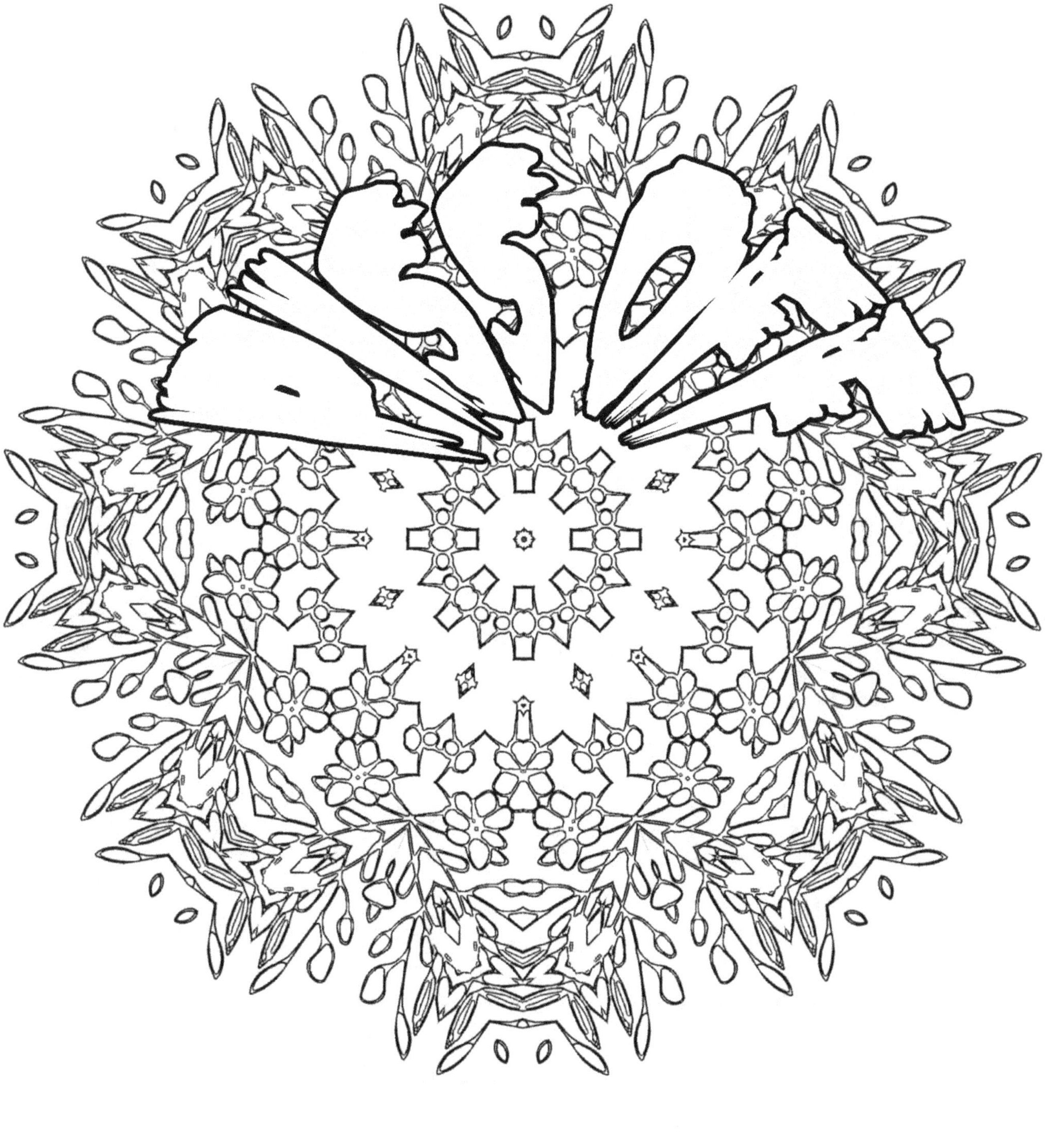

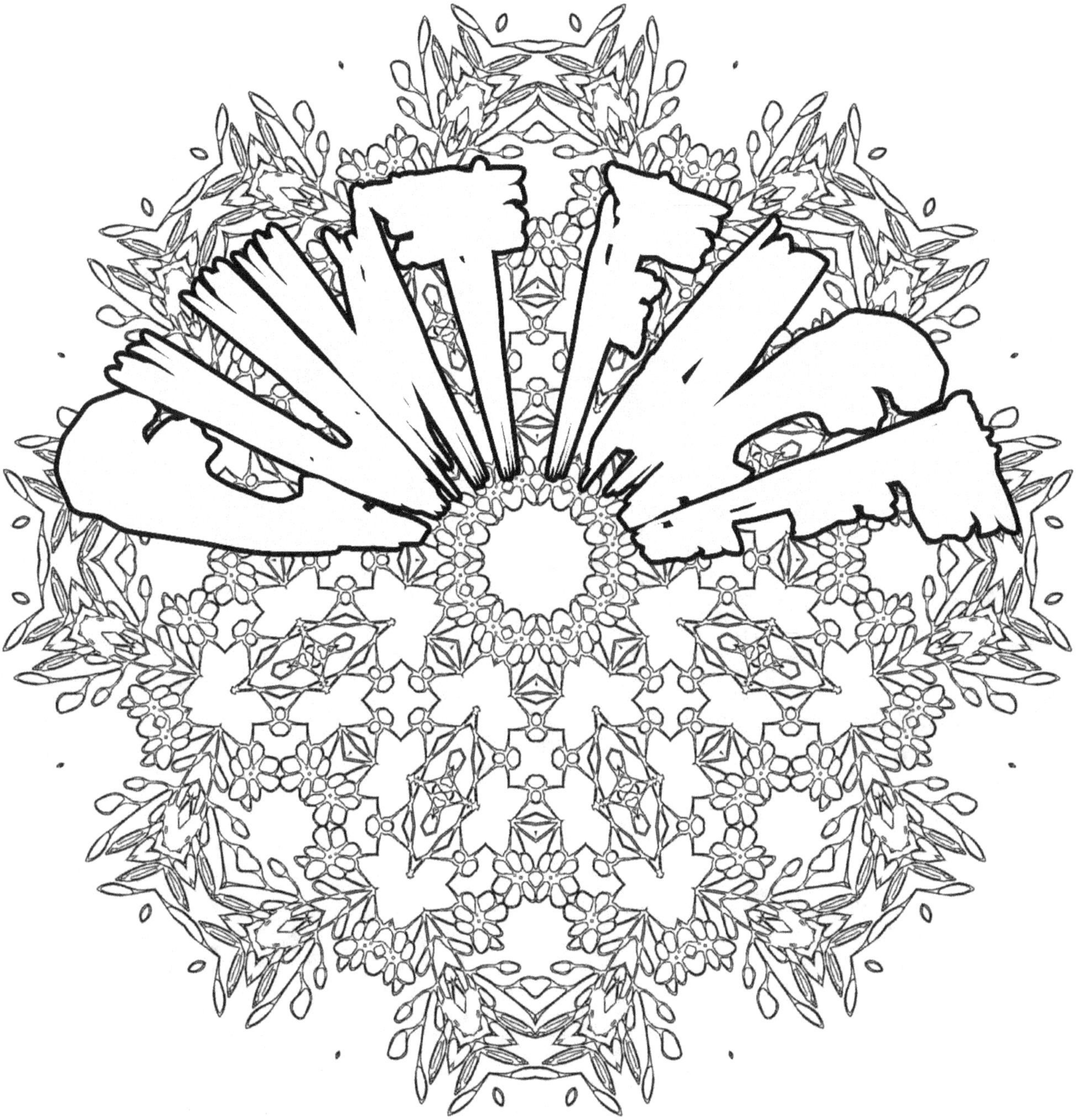

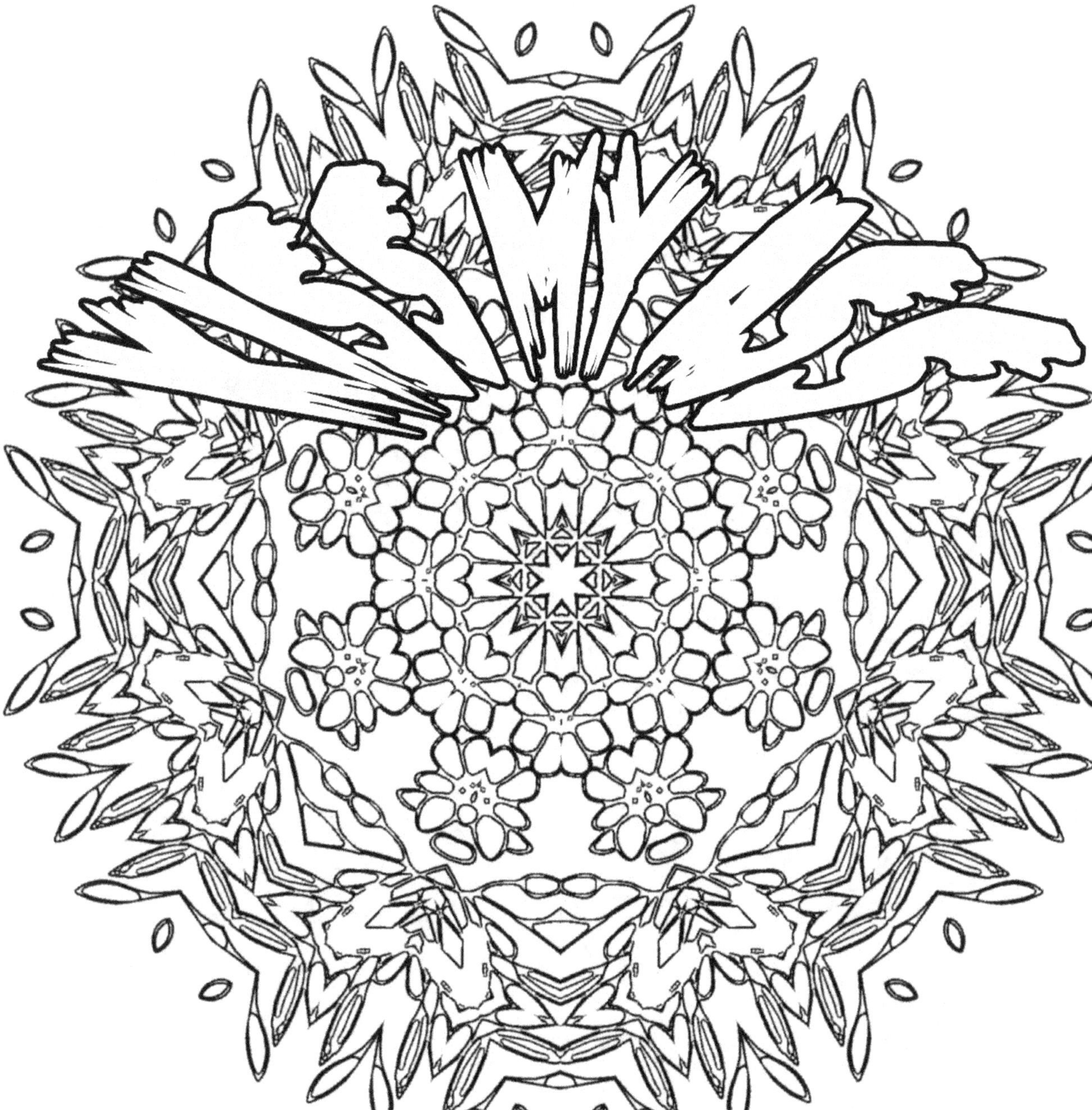

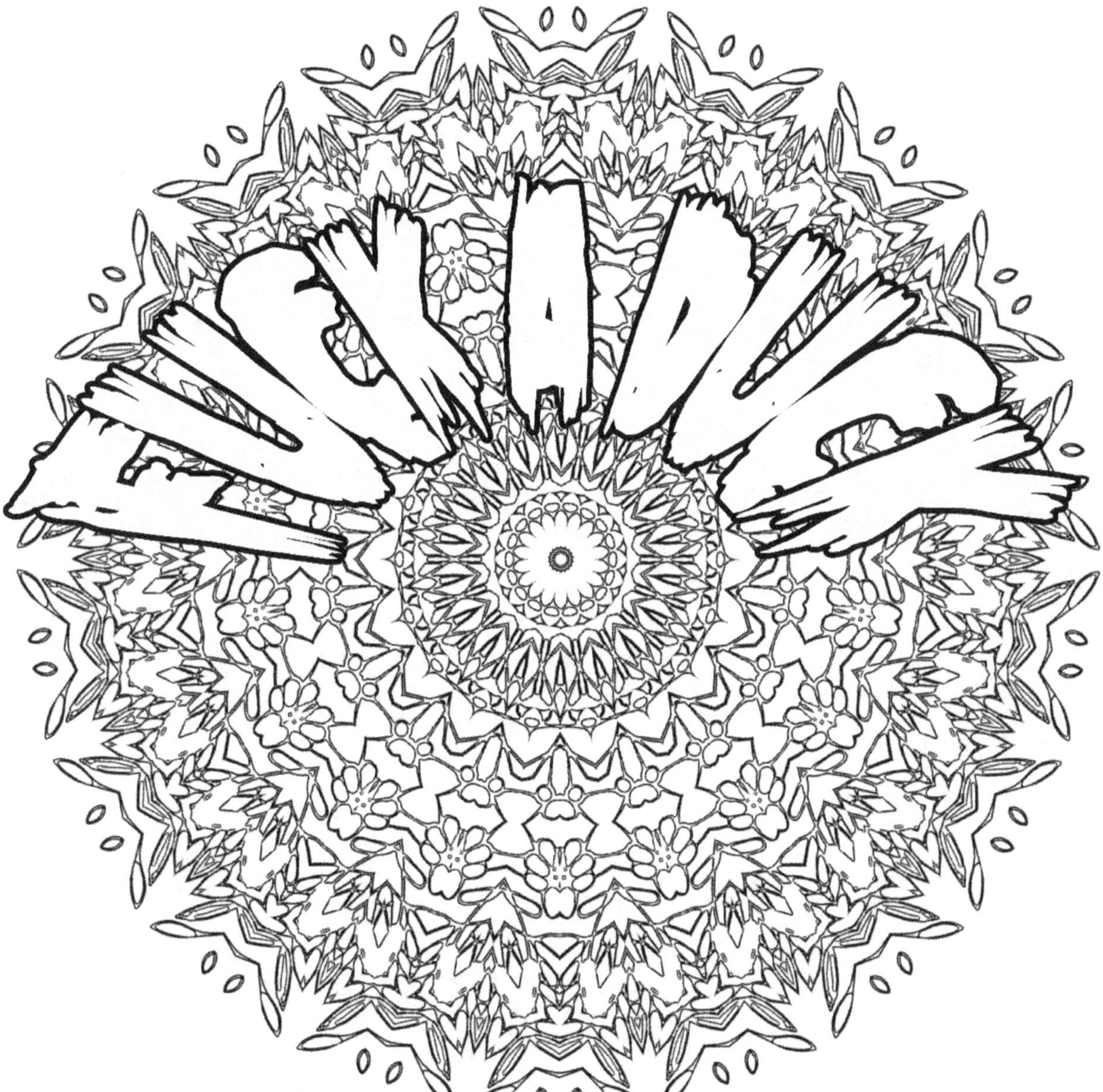

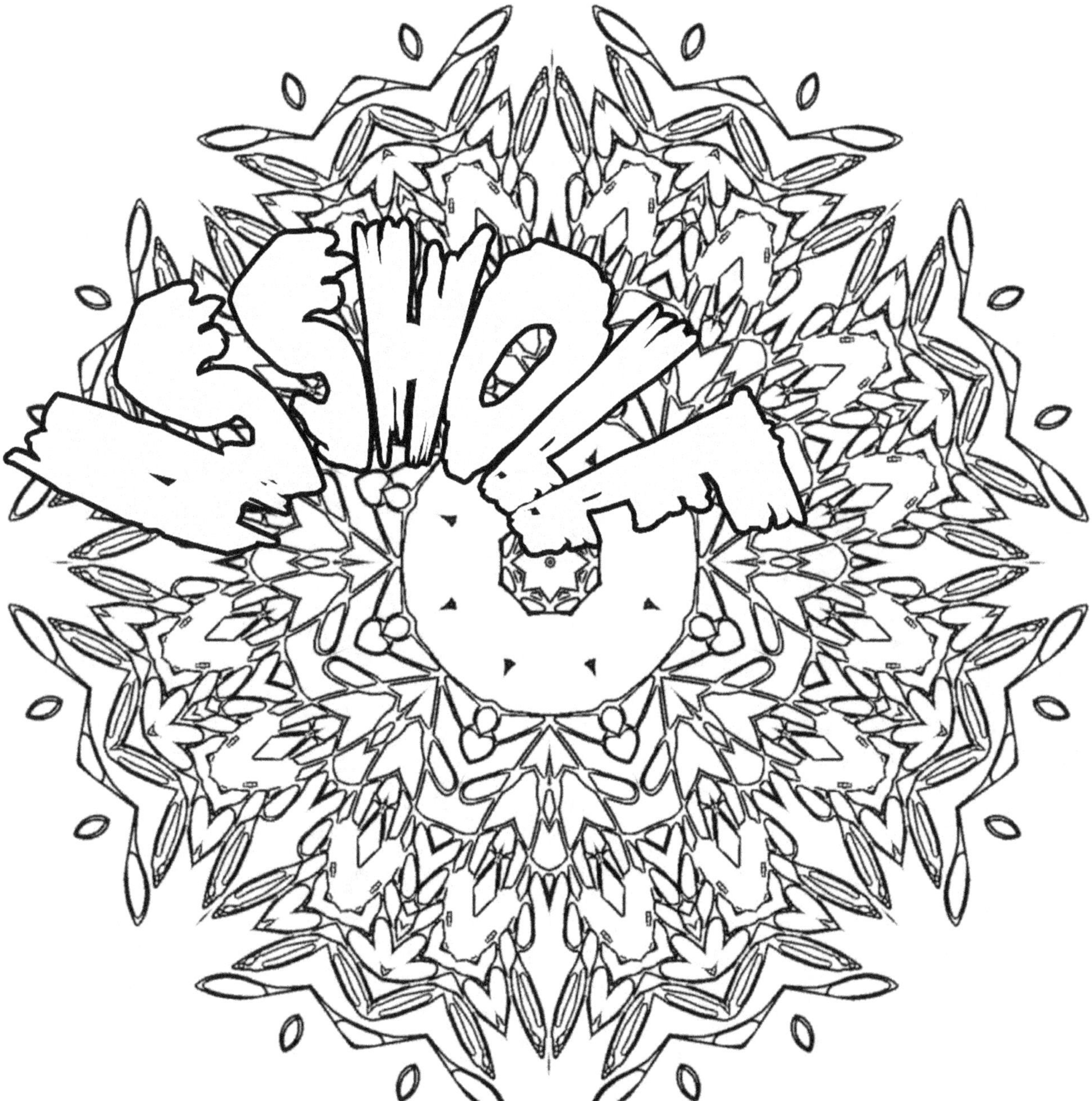
ASSHOLE

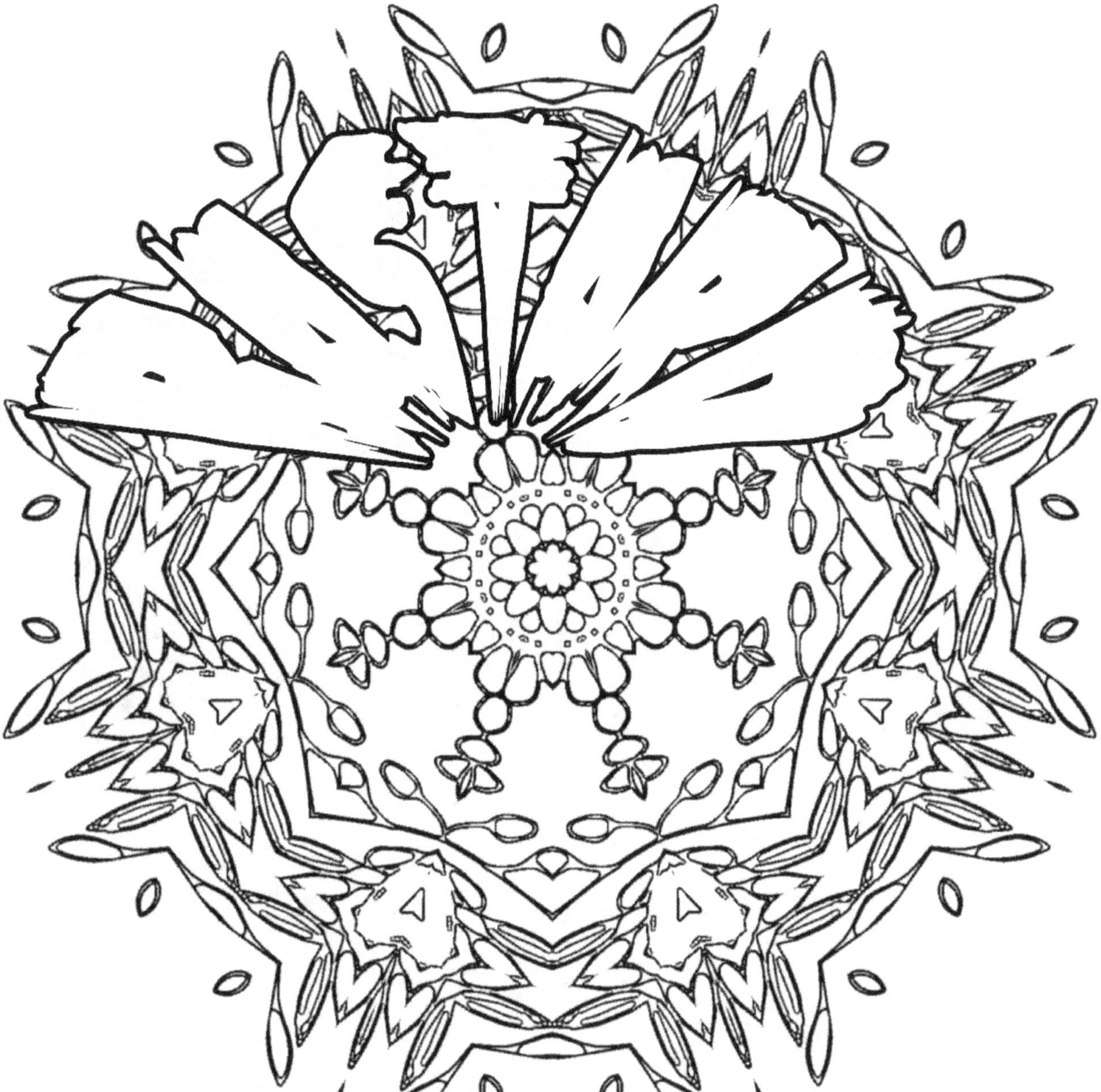

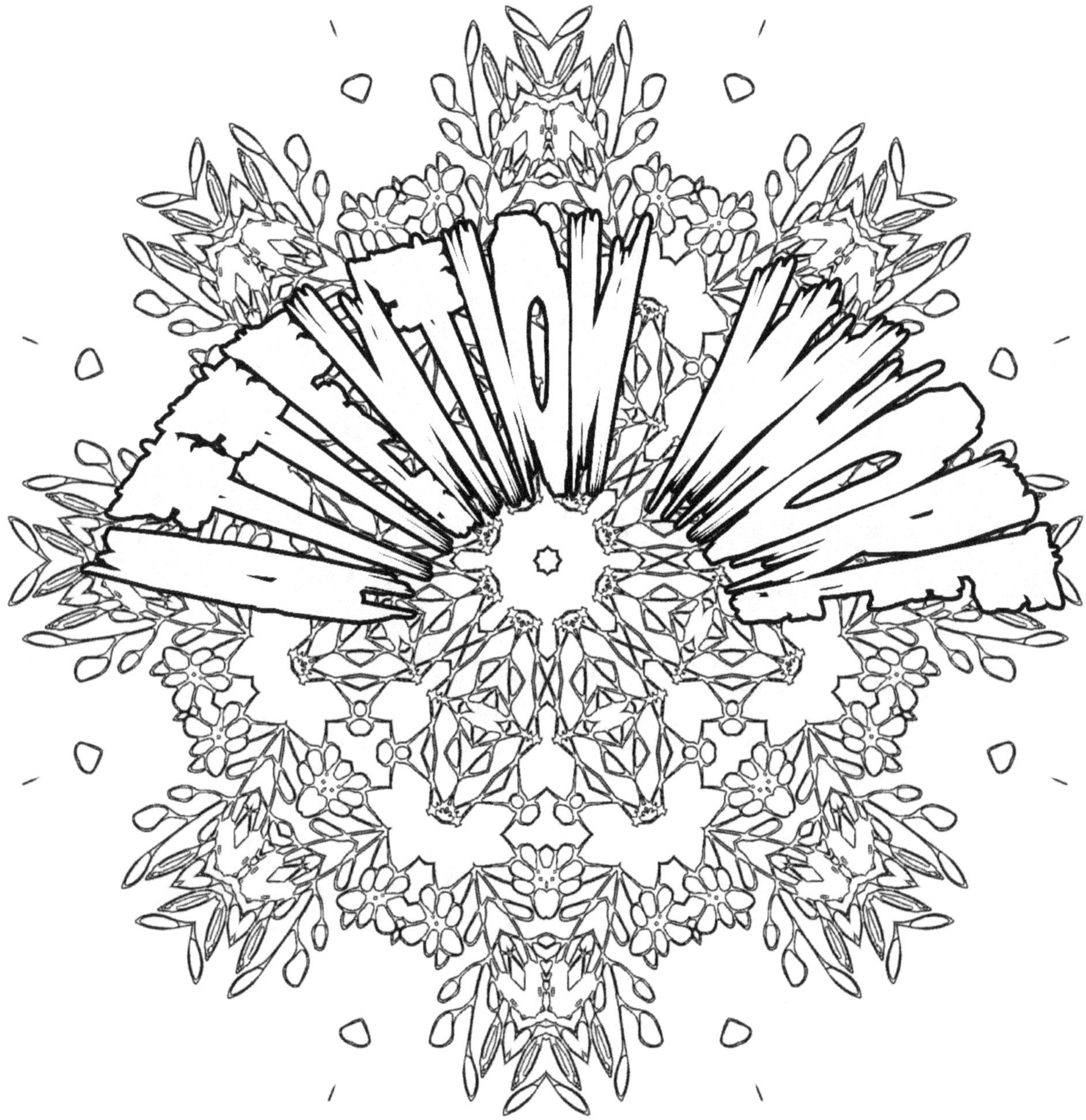

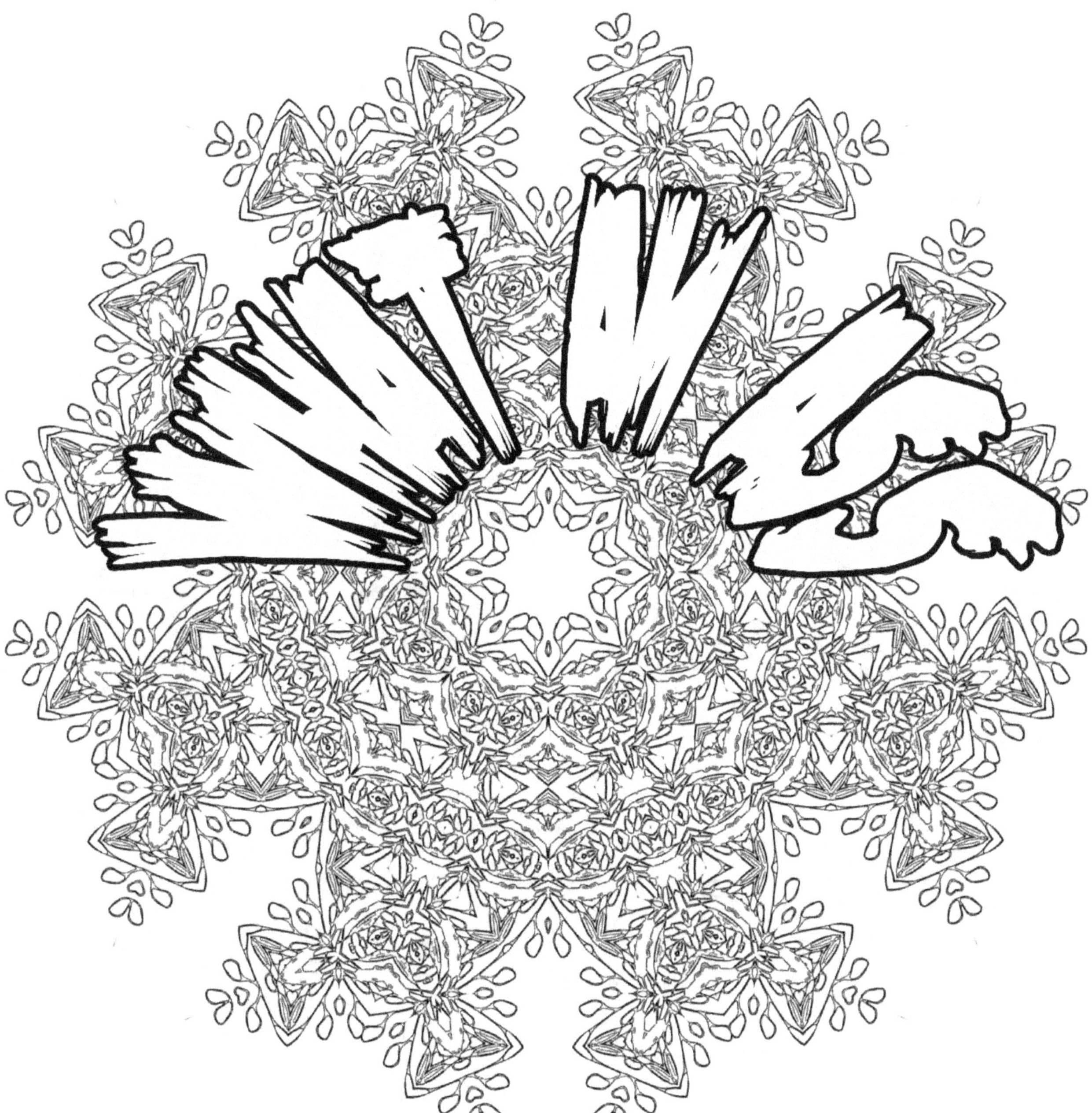

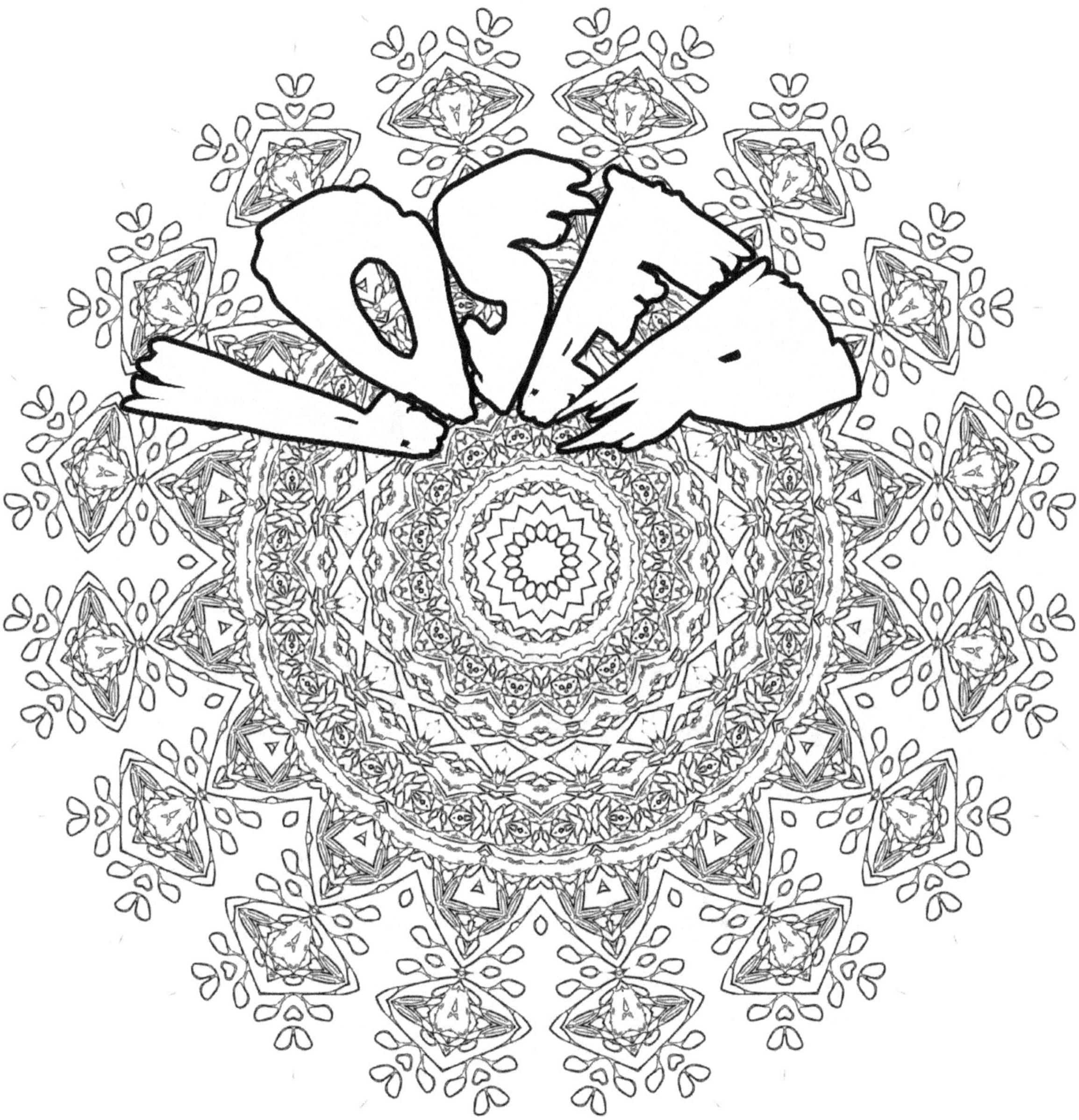

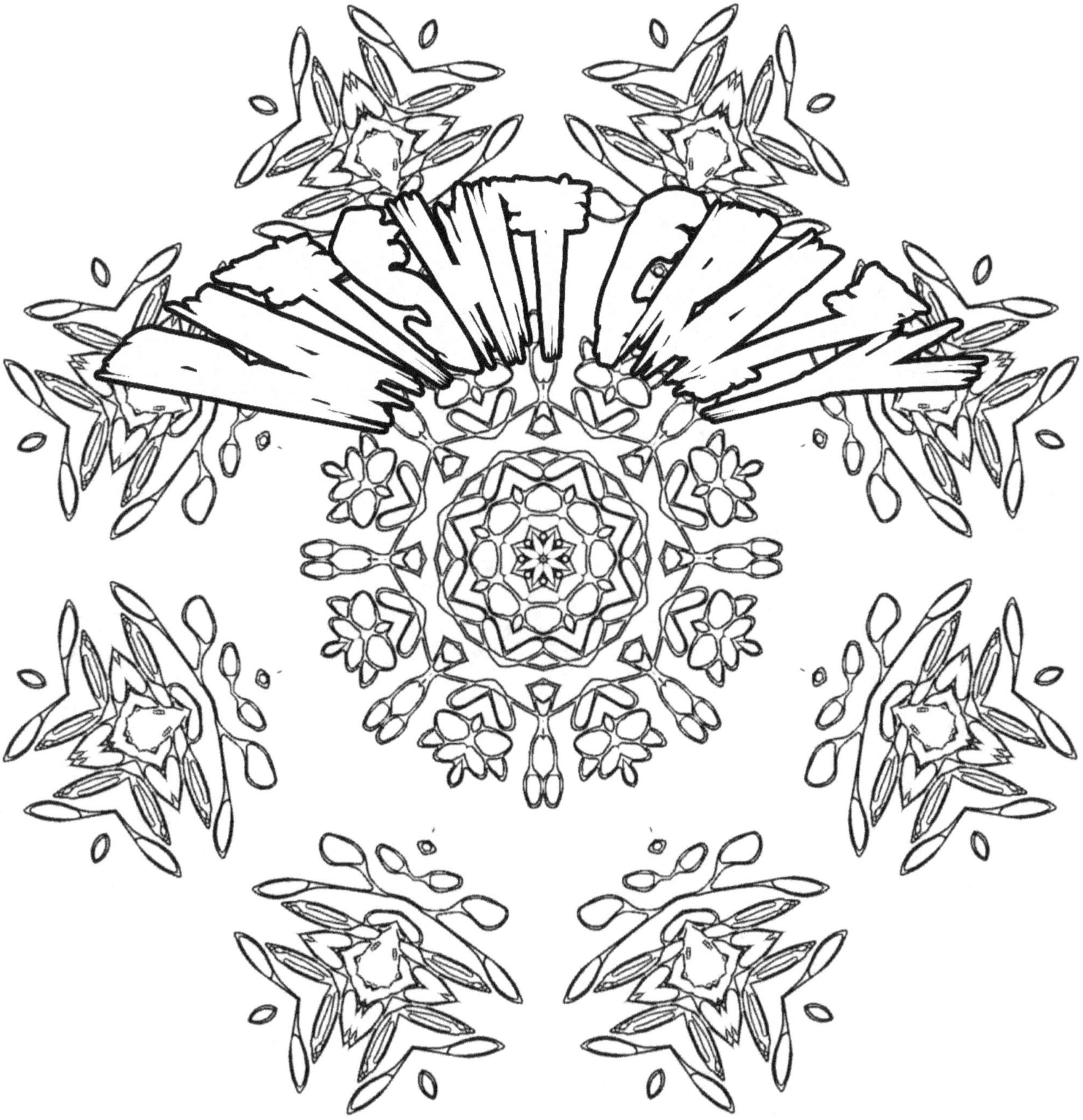
BATSHIT CRAZY

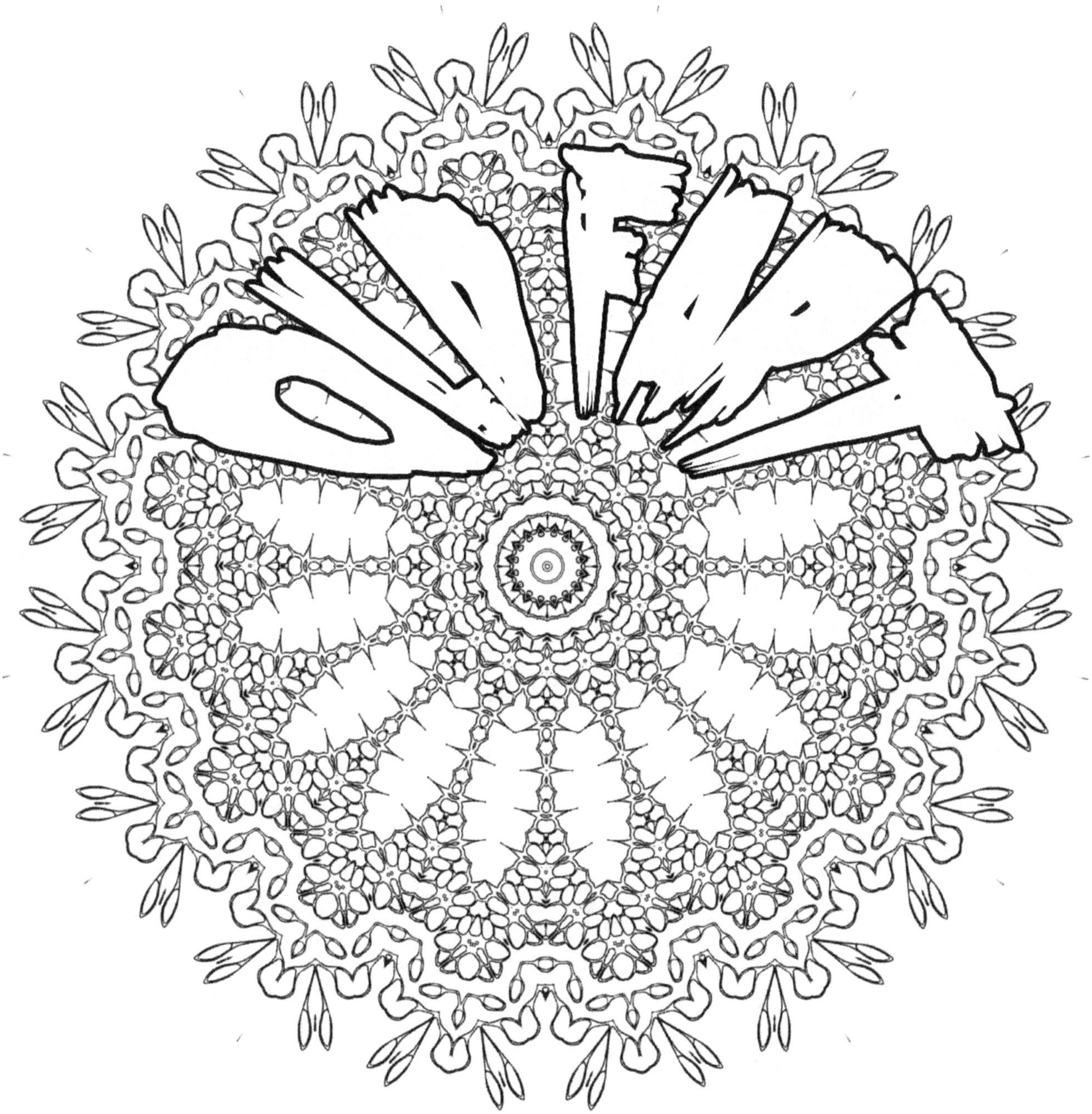
OLD FART

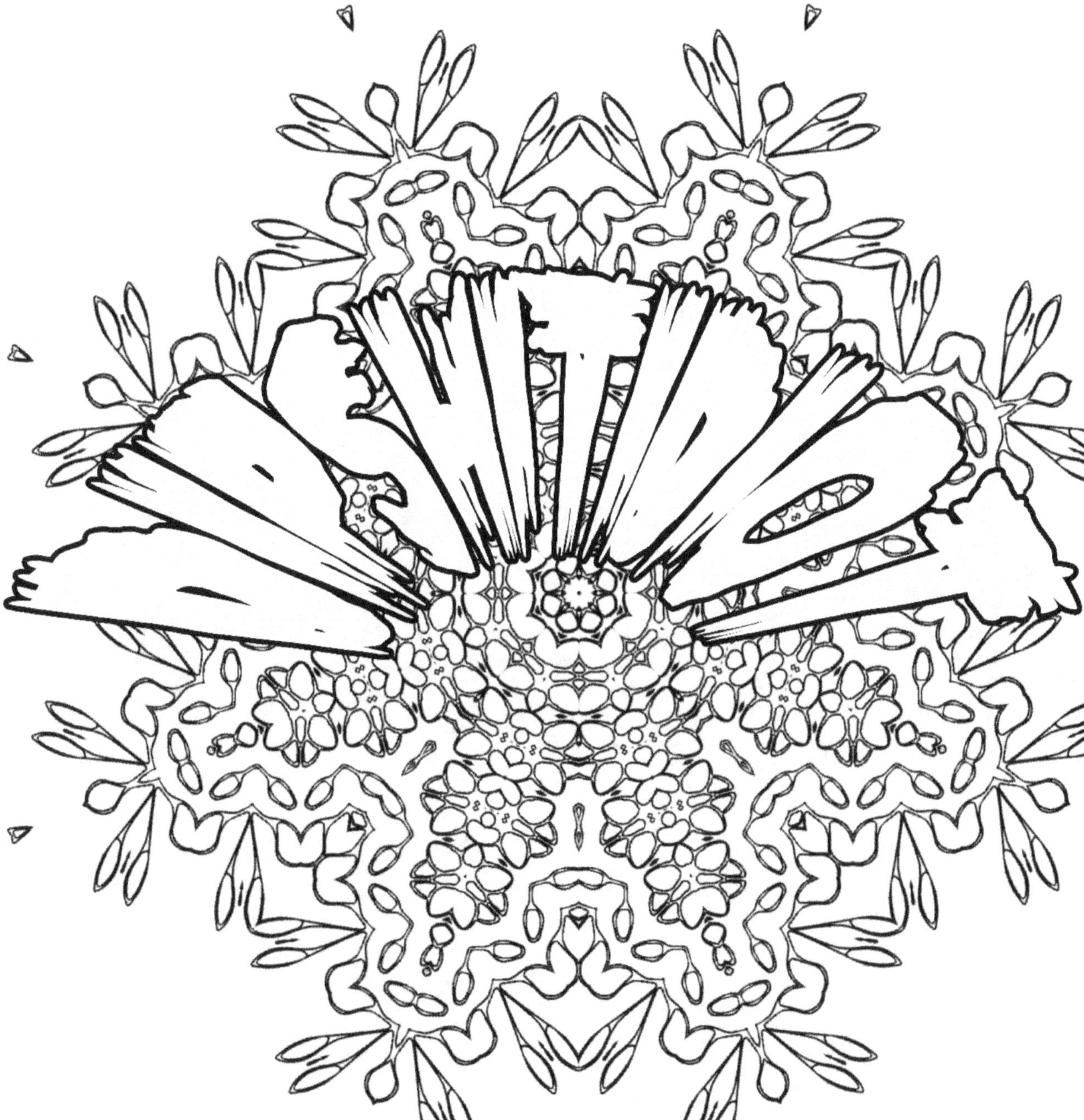

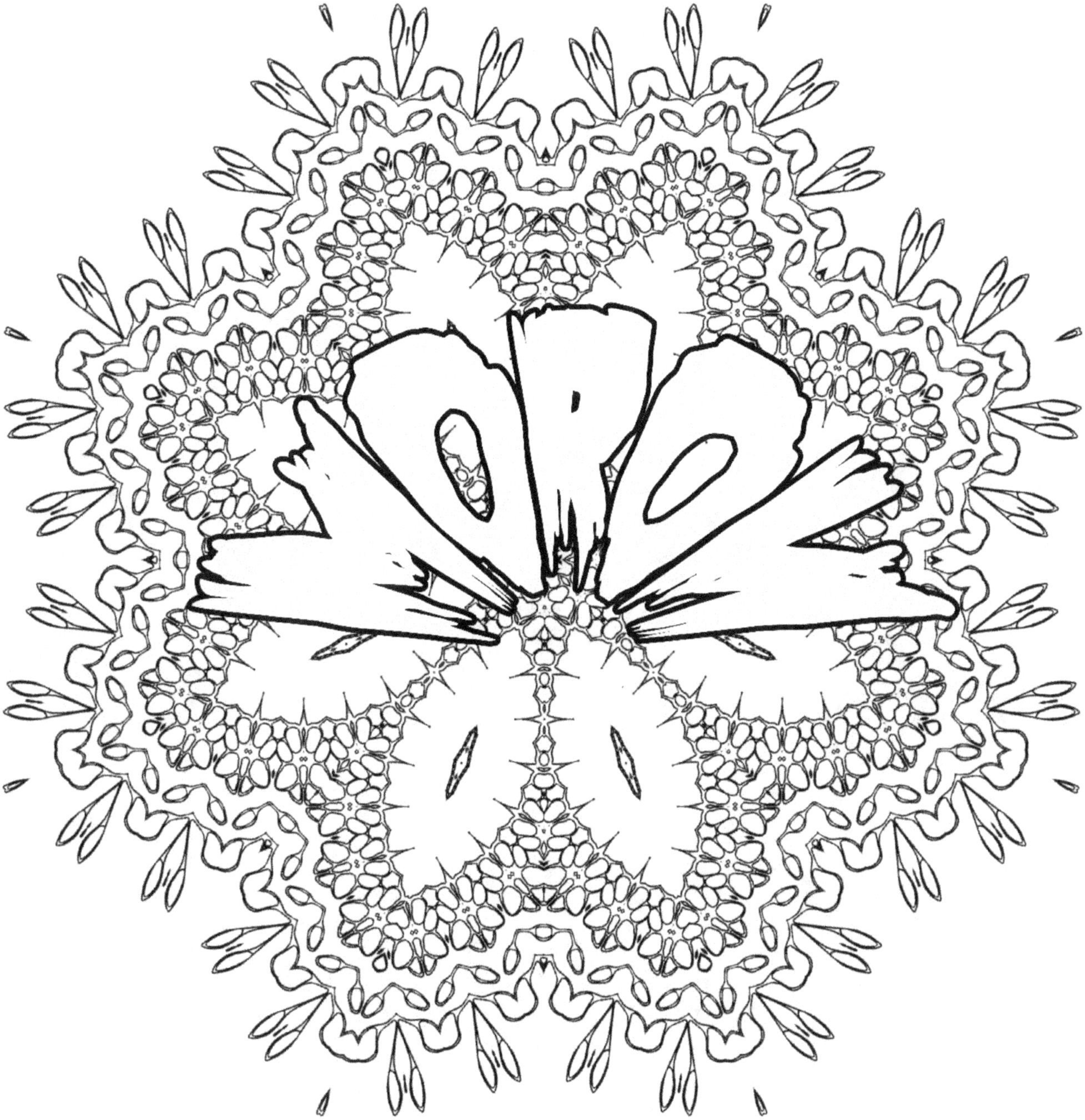

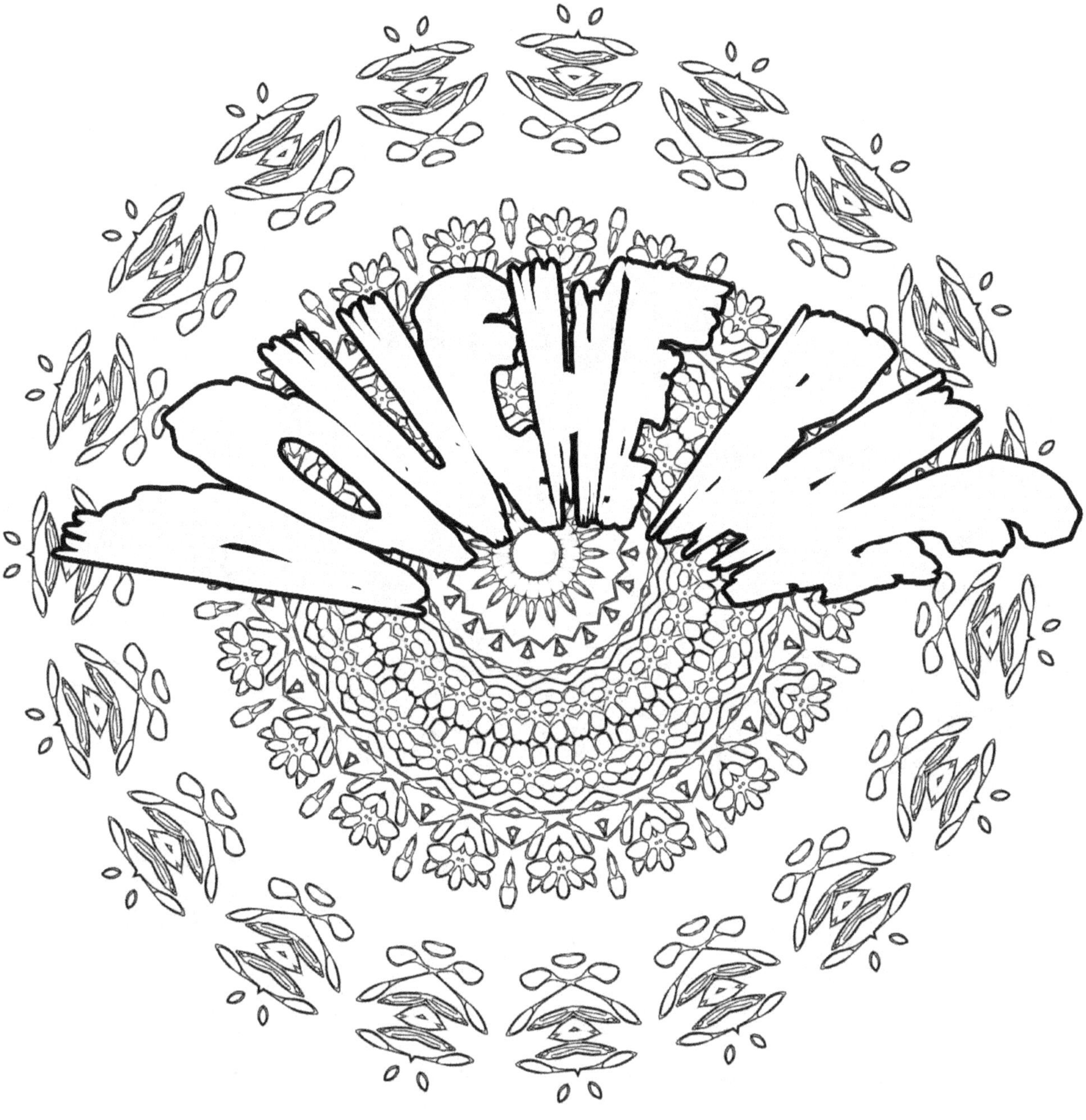
DOUCHEBAG

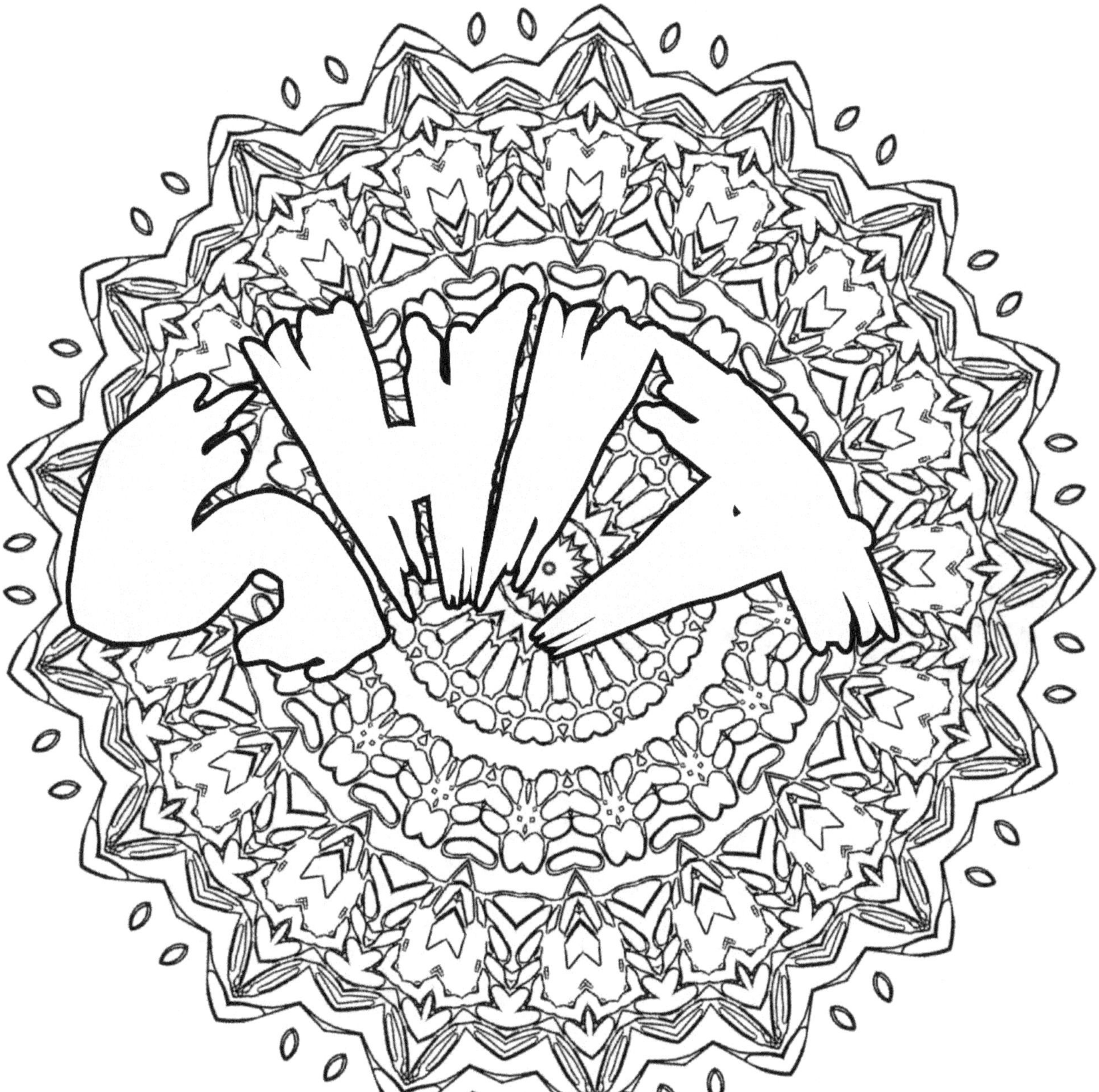

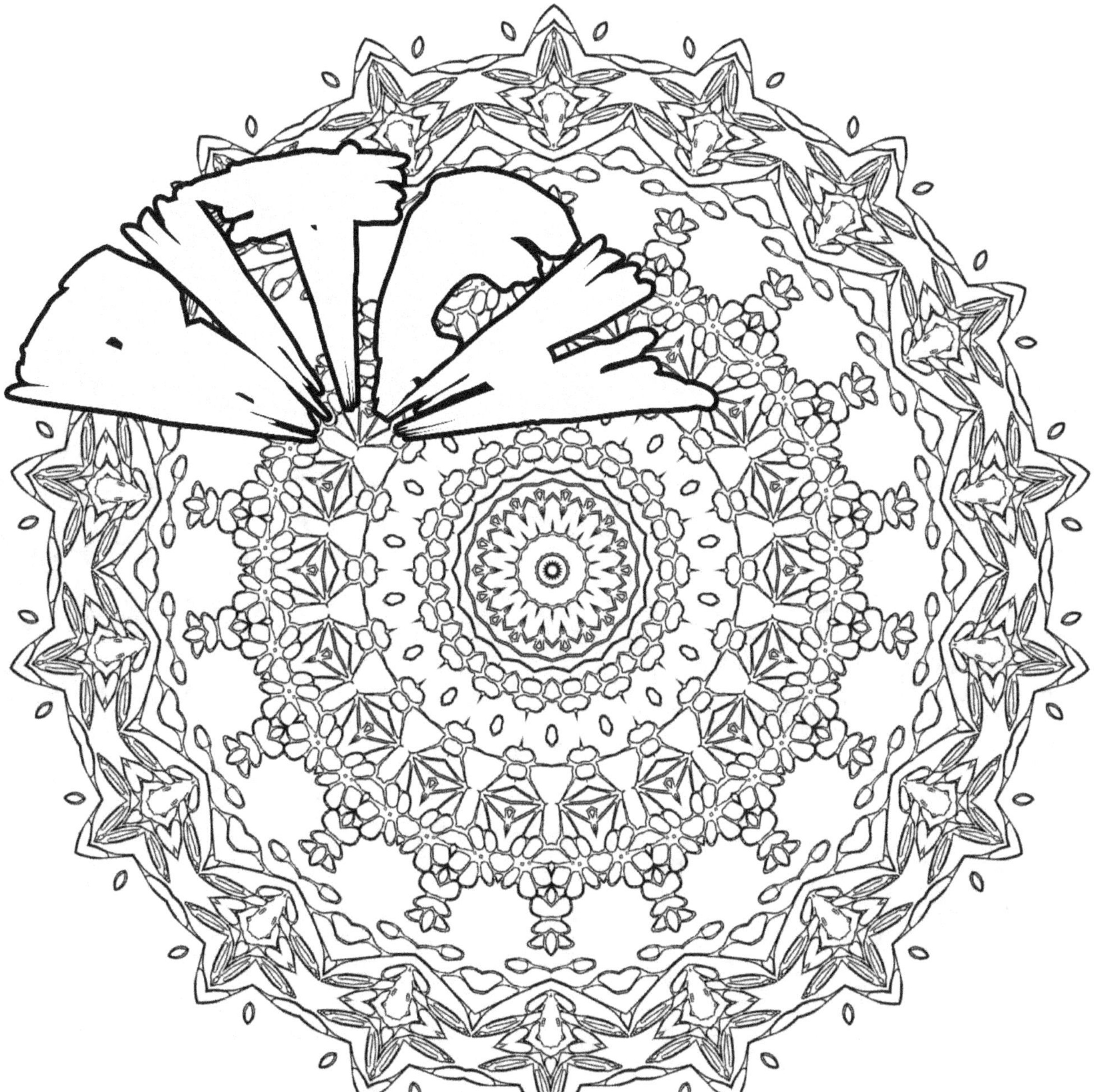

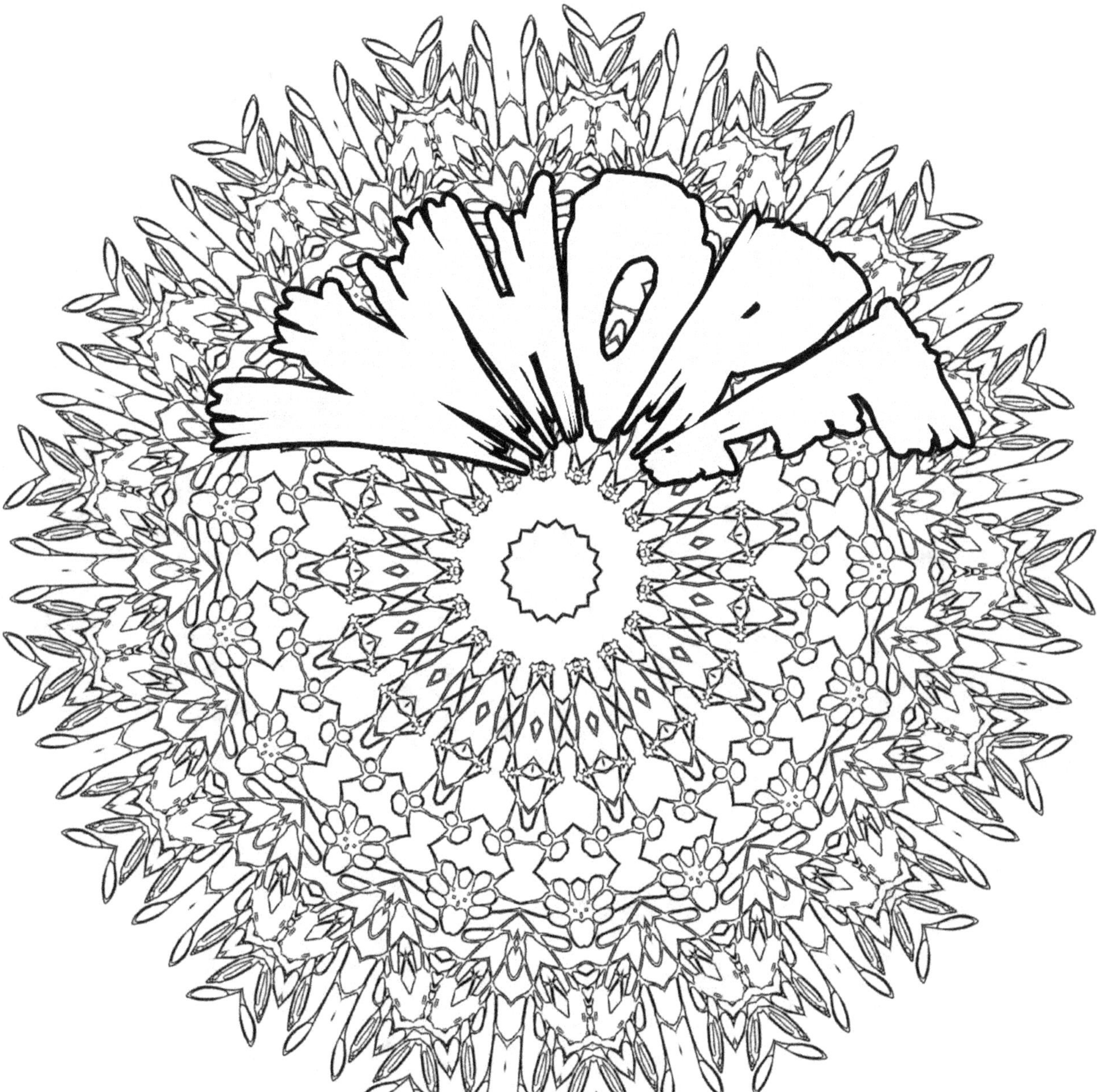
WHOA

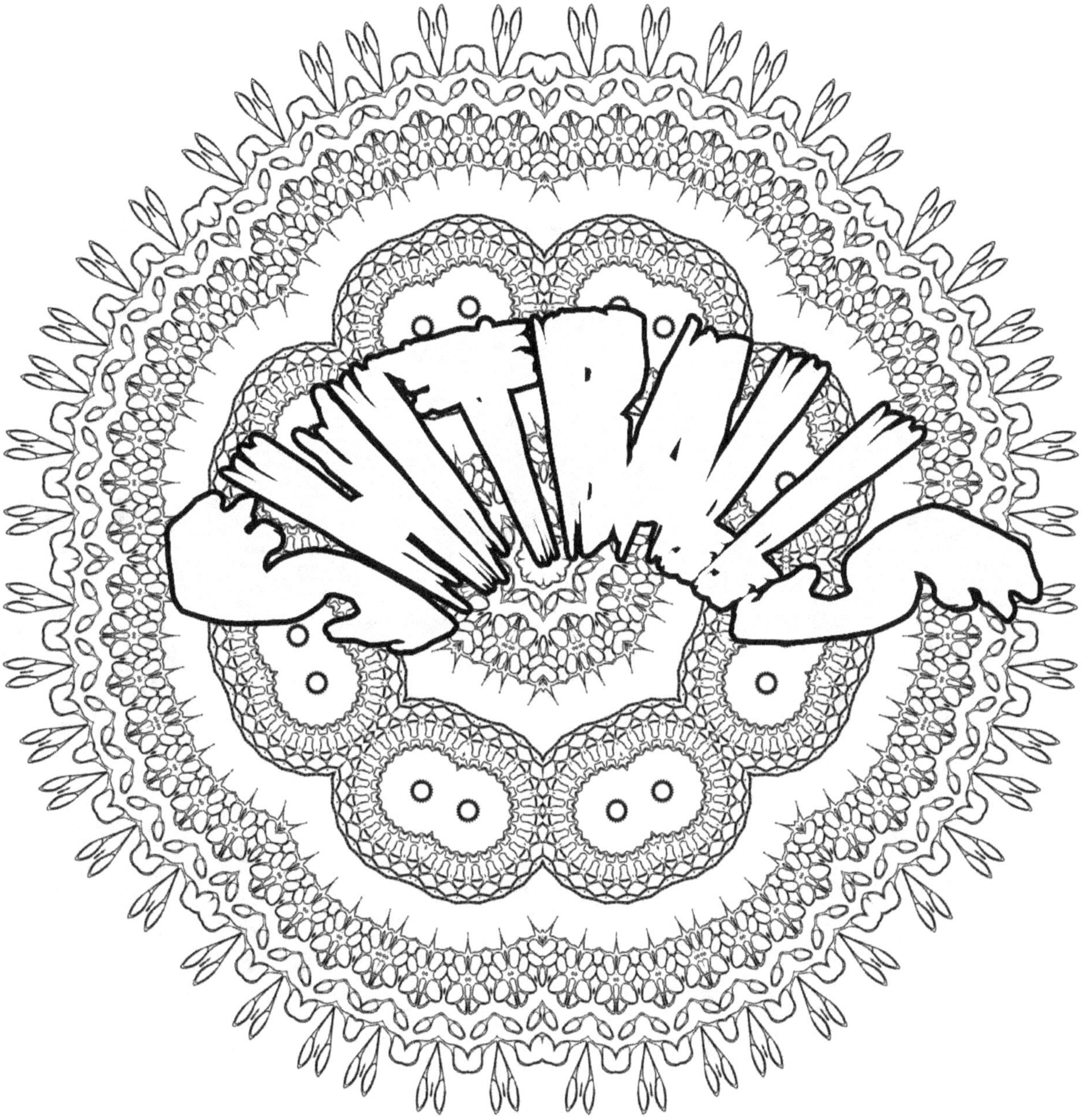

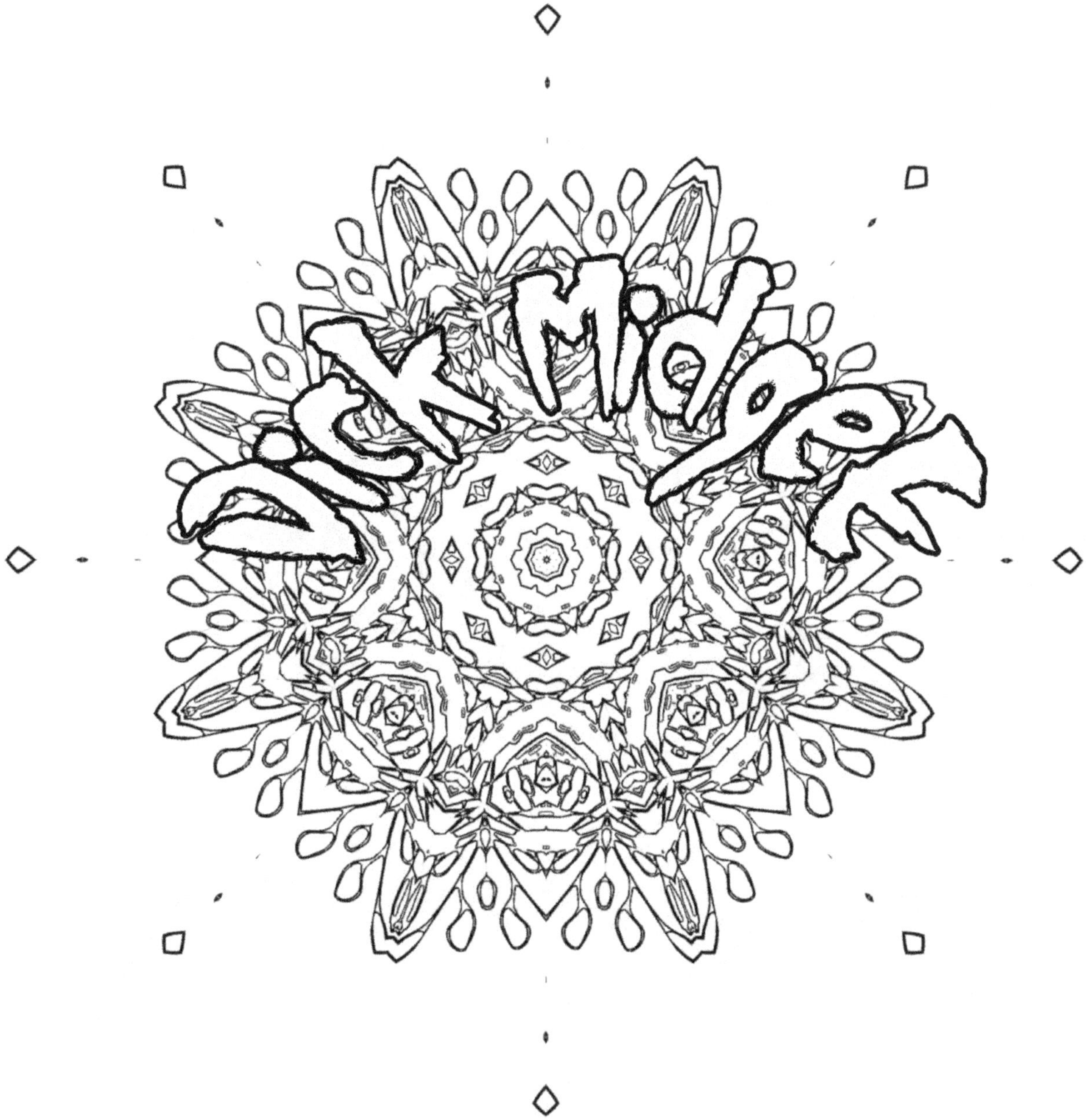
Dick Midget

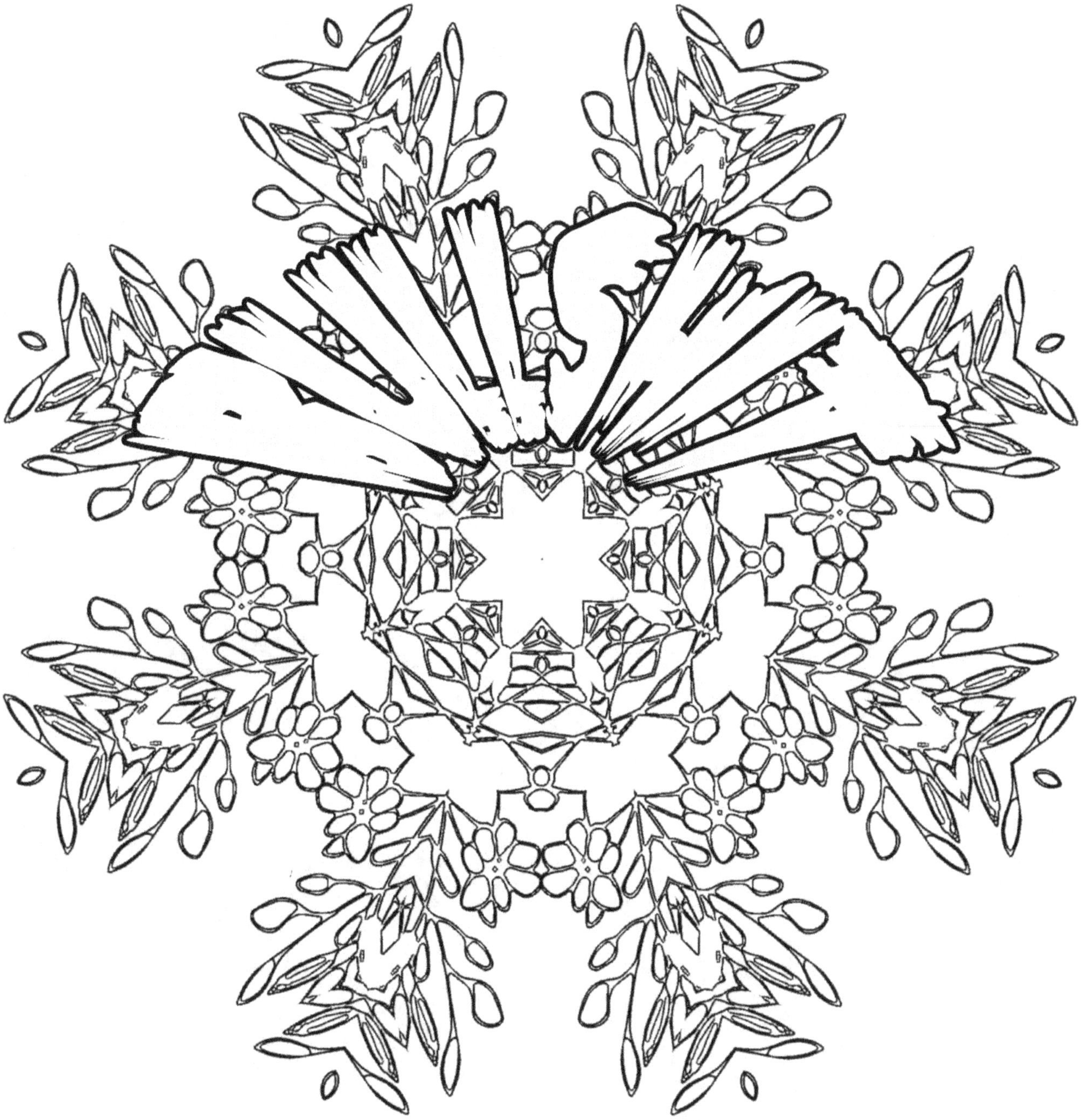

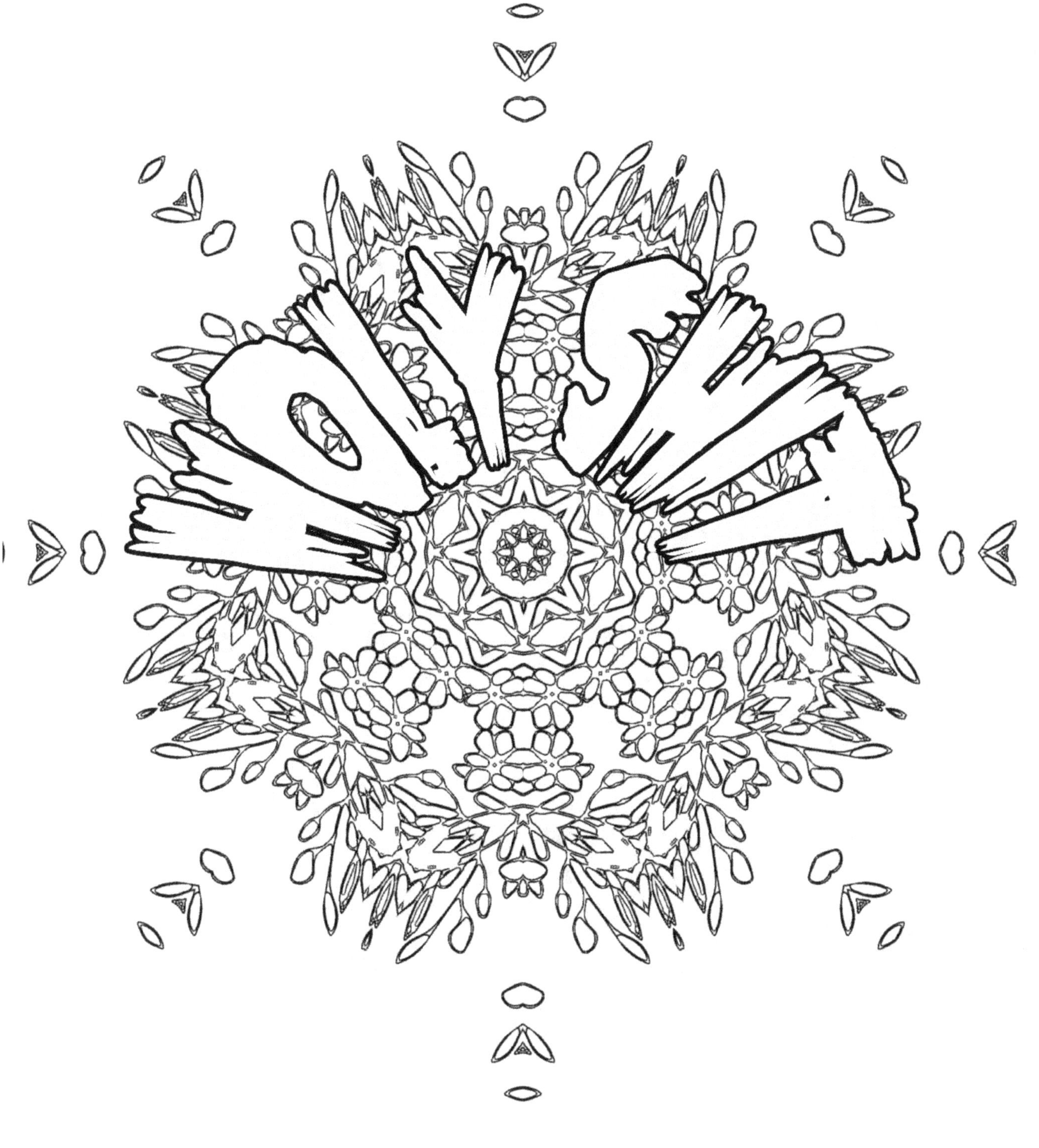
HOLY SHIT

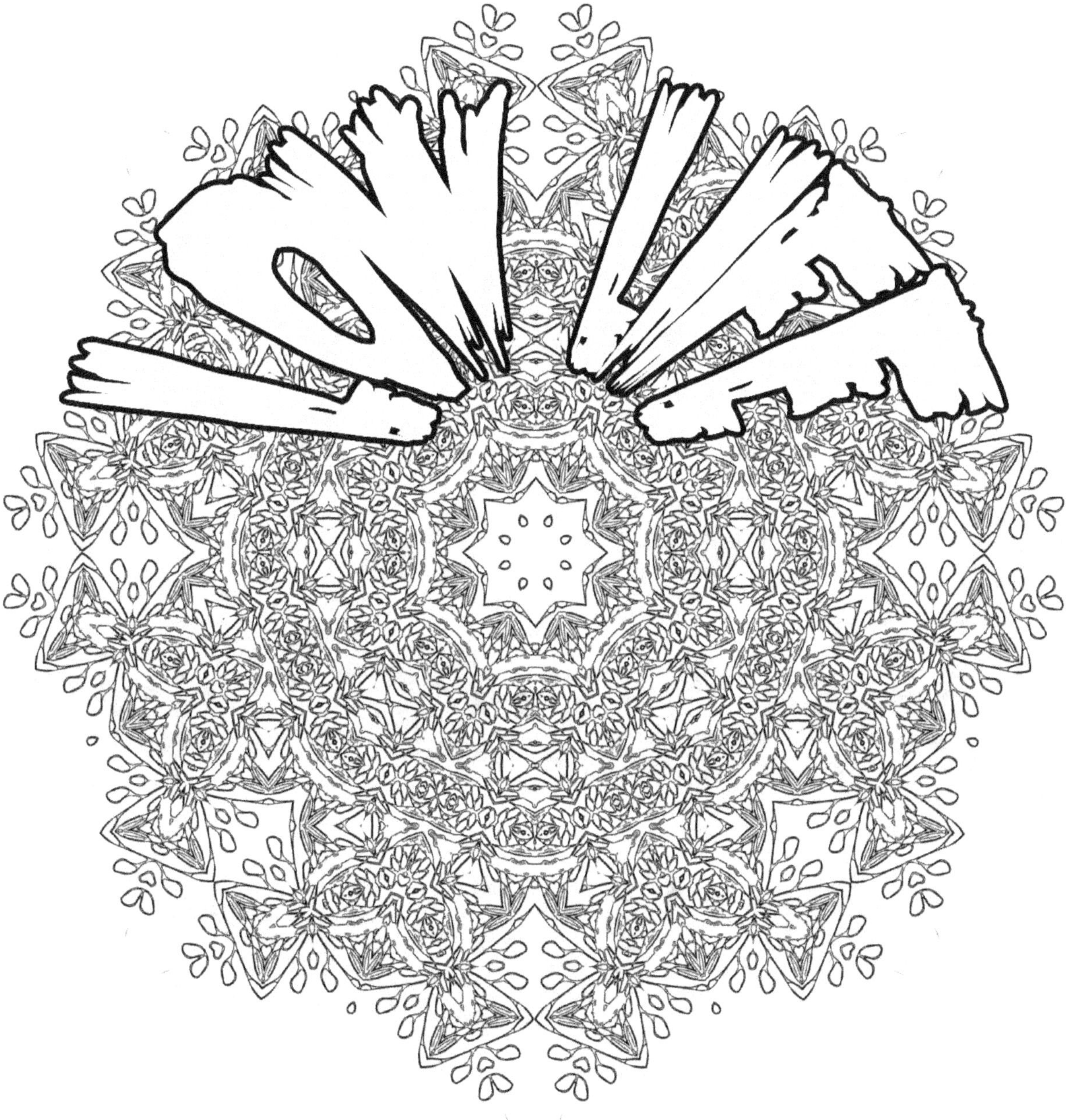

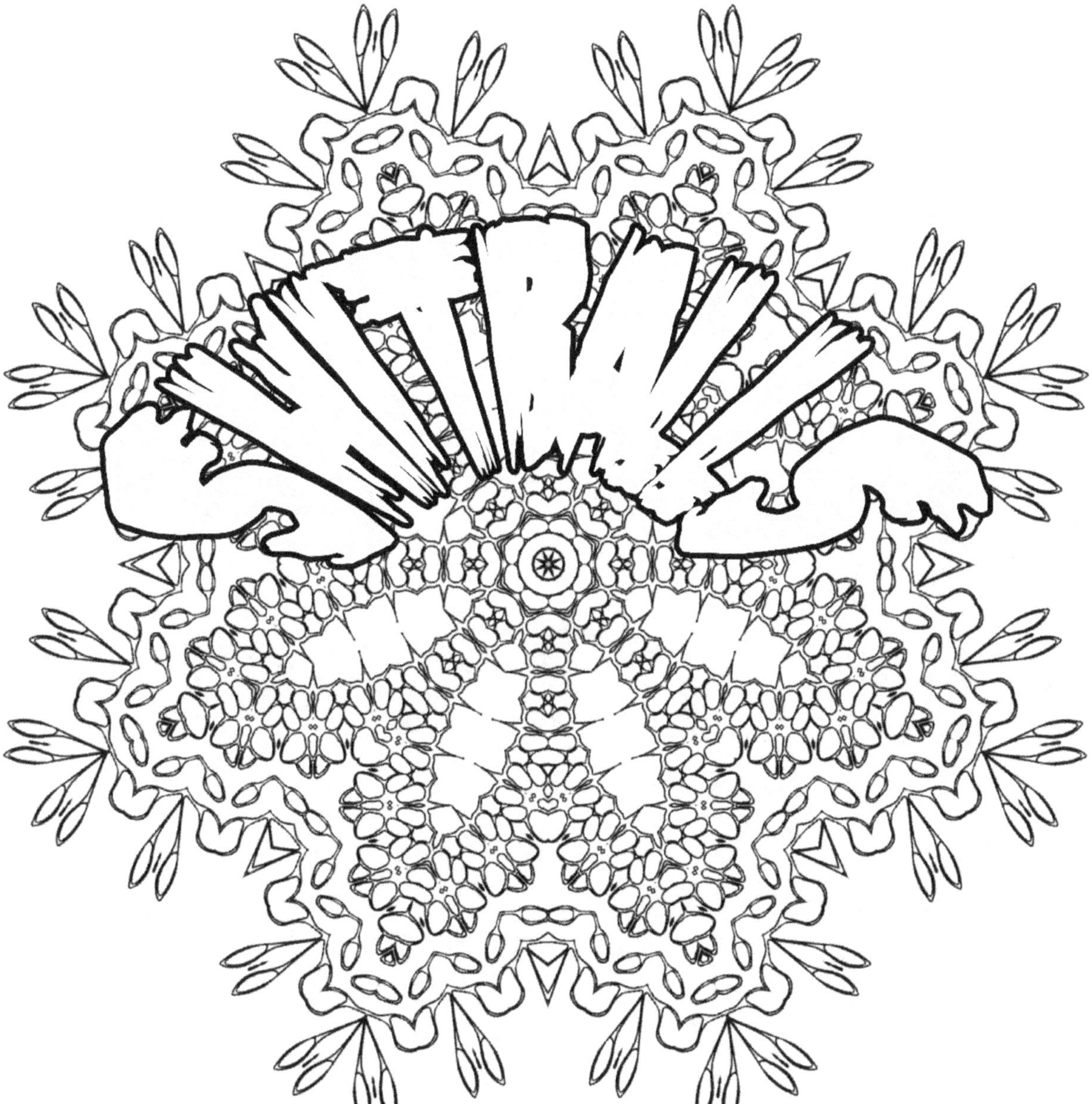

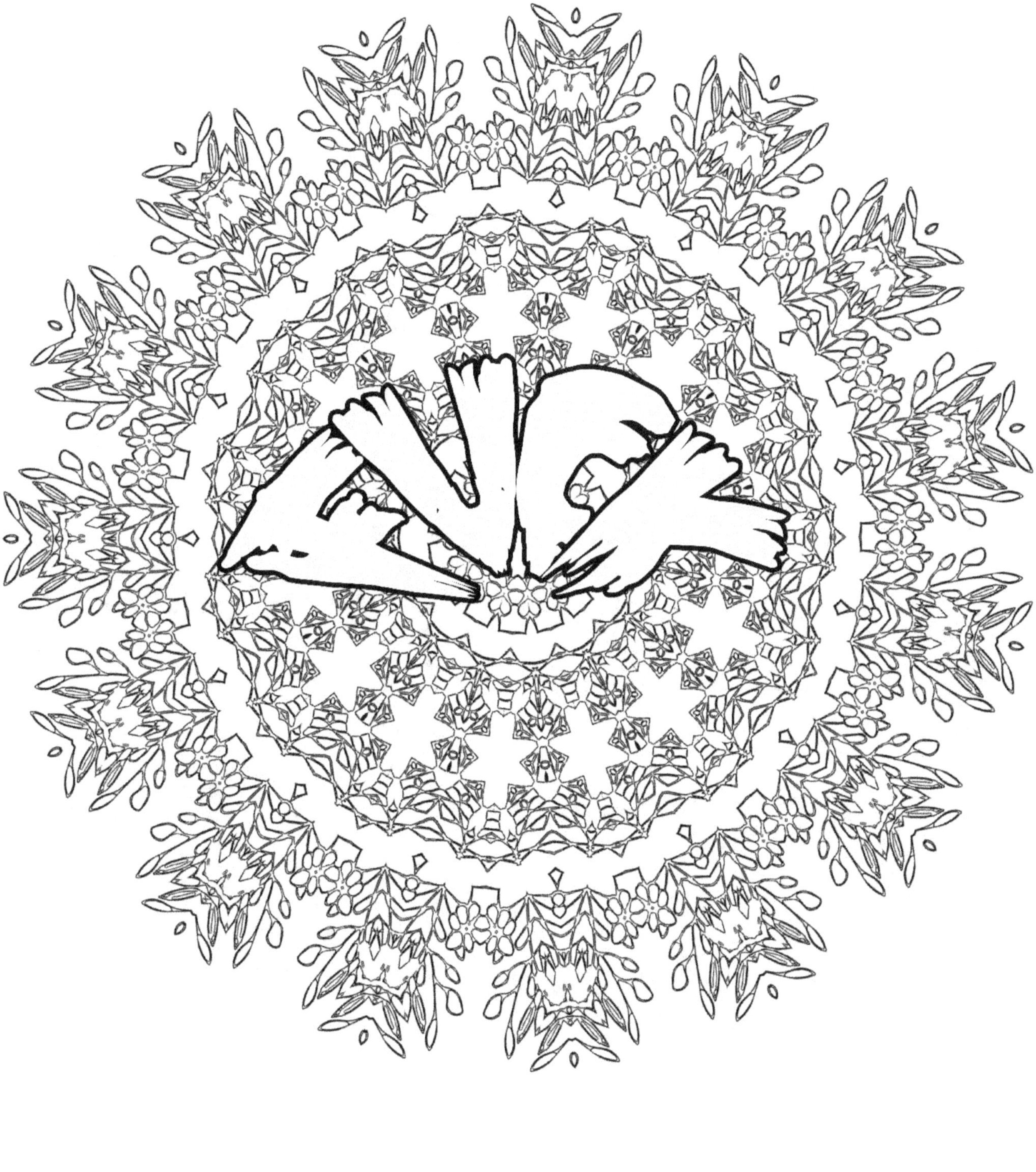

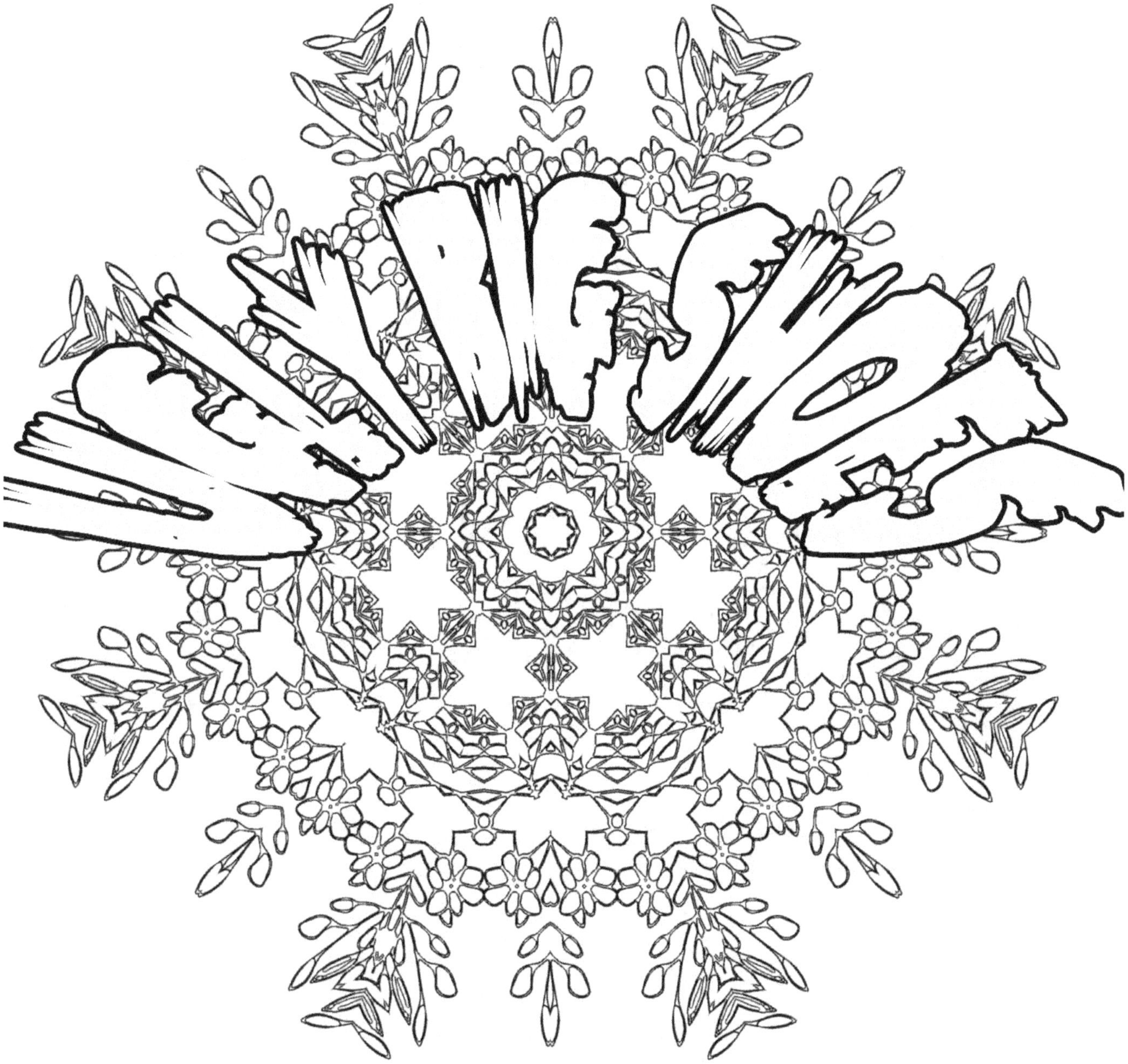
BIG SHOES

www.ingramcontent.com/pod-product-compliance
Lightning Source LLC
Chambersburg PA
CBHW081131180526
45170CB00008B/3072